START YOUR DAY WITH A GOOD NIGHT'S SLEEP

A Guide for Rest, Relaxation, and Blissful Sleep

ROBERT SACHS

START YOUR DAY WITH A GOOD NIGHT'S SLEEP
A GUIDE FOR REST, RELAXATION, AND BLISSFUL SLEEP

iUniverse books may be ordered through booksellers or by contacting:

iUniverse
1663 Liberty Drive
Bloomington, IN 47403
www.iuniverse.com
844-349-9409

ISBN: 978-1-5320-2658-4 (sc)
ISBN: 978-1-5320-2657-7 (e)

Library of Congress Control Number: 2017911528

Print information available on the last page.

iUniverse rev. date: 06/24/2023

ABOUT ROBERT SACHS

Robert Sachs is the author of *Tibetan Ayurveda: Health Secrets from the Roof of The World*, co-author of *Ayurvedic Spa* (with his wife, Melanie), and a number of other books covering such topics as oriental astrology, practical Buddhism, and conscious dying. His vision of an integrated, inter-dependent, and cooperative world is embodied in is book, *The Ecology of Oneness; Awakening in a Free World*.

Through his training as a clinical social worker, massage therapist, yoga teacher, and student of Tibetan Buddhism, Robert has studied and learned to master and teach forms of meditation, biofeedback, progressive relaxation, and yoga. His deep experience and appreciation for the value of sleep and deep rest is the inspiration behind this work.

Robert and his Beloved Melanie live on their urban farm on the California Central Coast.

MEDICAL DISCLAIMER

In this booklet, you will not learn about medications for sleep. These are too individual and should be considered with the help of whomever you see as your medical practitioner or consultant. My focus will be on what in Tibetan Ayurveda is clearly a part of the First Level of healing: lifestyle, including diet, exercise, hygiene, environmental considerations, relaxation and meditative practices. It is said that lifestyle is about ninety percent of what makes us feel dis-ease with what we are experiencing mentally and emotionally. First and foremost, we need to look at how we are living. If – as I said – you try to do as many of the things as I explain here – you will rest and sleep like a baby. For all those who need more, again, seek the advice of the professional in whom you have the most confidence.

ACKNOWLEDGEMENTS

The photos in this text were taken by Robert and Melanie Sachs. With the exception of the Taoist relaxation exercise, all of them first appeared in their book, *Ayurvedic Spa*, published by Lotus Press, 2007

CONTENTS

INTRODUCTION

The quality of your day – at least how you will face it - begins the night before. So, if you can remember, when was the last time you experienced a good night's sleep; when you woke up before the alarm, feeling refreshed and ready to meet the day – even before that morning coffee? On the other hand, how often do you struggle to find the snooze button on your alarm, eventually drag yourself into the shower, then to the coffee maker?

What we are about to share with you will not only change your idea of when your day starts, but It will also change how you think about both rest and sleep. Laying down flat, even fully passing out completely and becoming totally unconscious to your surroundings out of exhaustion or a chemically induced stupor or oblivion – whether through alcohol, recreational drugs, or ever-present and available legal prescriptions – is not necessarily, if ever, restful. You actually need to learn how to relax before you can really sleep. It is the combination of quality rest and great, undisturbed sleep that will give you the strength and energy to be with friends, family, on top of work, and in charge of your life.

Inadequate relaxation and rest, and poor quality sleep are a ubiquitous health concern and contribute to any number of major health problems in our bustling society. Depressed immunity, skeletal-muscular weakness that contributes to chronic pain, digestive and mood disorders, not to mention clinically defined insomnia are just some of the direct medical effects as well as being a major contributor to accidents in cars, at home, and in the work environment. Without quality rest and relaxation, you struggle through the day and lose the ability to perform at your natural best. If you are at all concerned about how you look, there are the telltale signs of poor quality rest and the resulting strain that one can try to conceal with more cosmetics, even surgery; vain attempts to mask puffiness and bags around the eyes, sagging in the cheeks and around the mouth. But, not only are a lack of quality rest, relaxation, and sleep hard on your body, your appearance, mind, and personal effectiveness. The money it takes to pep you up during the day and put you down to sleep at night affects the pocketbook. If you watch any TV or listen to drive-time radio in the morning and early afternoon, think of all the ads for coffee and caffeinated drinks. And, as you get to the evening time, there are the ads for beer, wine, and a host of prescribed and over-the-counter sleep medications. The bottom line is that sleeplessness is big business! All at your expense.

But, you can change that.

According to the ancient holistic system of Asia known as Ayurveda, sleep is the "wet nurse of the world," because it is nurturing, nourishing, and regenerating. There are two types of sleep, both of which in combination contribute to a quality night's rest; (1) deep dreamless sleep that restores the physical body and (2) active dreaming sleep called REM (Rapid Eye Movement) sleep that helps clear the mind of conflicting emotions. In a good night's rest, we experiences each of these sleep states. As we spend nearly a third of our lives sleeping, it is so vital to make our sleep the great healer and strengthener it has the potential to be. At the same time, it is possible to get some of these same benefits in times of rest and relaxation during the day. In this booklet, therefore, not only will you learn how to sleep well. You will also learn how to do effective brief progressive relaxation techniques that will help you to recharge your batteries during the day.

What Contributes to Poor Rest?

There are many factors that can contribute to poor quality rest and a tendency to develop insomnia. As you look at this list, be aware that the more factors that you can identify with, the greater the likelihood that you are not getting quality rest.

- First and foremost, tension and worry. These can have both physical and emotional causes. Simply put, if your mind is stirring with too many thoughts or undigested emotions, your rest will be agitated, your dreams chaotic, and the result of your night thrashing about - exhaustion.
- Routines and lifestyle patterns that keep you up consistently after midnight.
- Finding yourself catching up on sleep with long naps during the day, which in turn creates problems when bedtime comes – a vicious cycle. We shall discuss this more at length when we talk about optimal times for sleep.
- Eating late at night or eating foods that are very stimulating to the body and mind, such as garlic, coffee, chili, alcohol. Yes, even though alcohol is considered a sedative, if you drink too much or at a certain point in the night, your blood sugar can go up, and then plummet, creating a hypoglycemic (low blood sugar) reaction that can make you restless.
- Sleeping in an environment that is not conducive to quality rest. This can include:
  - a bed that is too hard or soft for your body

- too much light in the room
- too much noise
- electro-magnetic interference, such as synthetic sheets and blankets, heating pads left on as you sleep, an electric clock radio beside the bed, your computer, TV, and cell phone.

The Goal of this booklet

The goal of this booklet is to help you eliminate these various causes and conditions to the best of your ability to achieve the best possible quality of rest and sleep for you. Knowing how hard, but essential it is to make lifestyle and attitudinal changes, the journey I shall take you through in this book begins with the external factors, like the physical attributes of your rest and sleep environment (bedding, etc.), then direct you inward to the changes of body, mind, and emotions that will not only help you to sleep better. They will change your life for the better overall.

Like we said, it is usually not just about one thing, but a variety and combination of factors coming together like a perfect storm that keeps your night turbulent. Our personal habits – what we chose to eat, do, and include in our lives are the easiest things to change, but more often than not, they are last things we actually want to change. At the same time, we can't necessarily move or avoid those things that have to do with environmental factors. So, as the old Buddhist adage says -"It is easier to put on shoes than to cover the world in leather" - we need to come up with solutions and changes that work with our situation and our minds – and hopefully be effective.

The insights and recommendations in this book come from a number of disciplines; my training as a yoga teacher, in Western naturopathic methods and the oriental medical disciplines including Macrobiotics and Ayurveda, as a biofeedback practitioner, my studies of Feng Shui, and my work as a clinical social worker and massage therapist.

From this eclectic mix of wisdom on rest and sleep, the more of these factors, both personally and environmentally, you can address, the greater the likelihood of your success. This booklet IS about solutions. So, relax, read, and apply. This is the strategy that will work best in getting you the rest and sleep you want and need.

CHAPTER ONE

Your Sleep Environment

Drawing upon the list of factors that contribute to challenging your rest and sleep as listed in the Introduction, let's go through the points and areas of focus in the opposite order and give you solutions that will give you a quality night's rest. In particular, this chapter will focus primarily on your sleeping environment.

Let's start with your bed

There are an endless number of theories as to what kind of mattress or sleep surface is best for you; waterbeds, memory foam, air beds, hard surfaces, soft surfaces, even planks of wood. Some of what will work for you depends on your age and the physical condition of your neck and spine. If your spine and neck are well aligned and healthy, then you can take more liberty in finding out what surface feels best for you. But, if you have neck and spinal misalignments, sometimes the softer, more accommodating surfaces may initially feel good, but they can also reinforce and lock you into the misalignments, thus cause greater pain down the road.

Regardless of what kind of sleep surface you have, buy or use a bed that is **off the ground**, i.e. the mattress is not directly on the ground and/or has a proper frame with legs. This advice comes from the Feng Shui tradition of the East. The reasons, however, are, for the most part, quite practical. First, if your mattress is directly on the ground, it is colder, will attract more dust, and may get damp, even moldy on the under surface without you even knowing it. Secondly, a mattress on the ground is harder to get up out of. Rather than simply roll over and put your feet on the ground, you have to use a variety of muscles that have yet to get warmed up. This may be fine when you're young or when you are camping. But, for daily comfort and to feel more rested, up off the ground is what is recommended here.

1

Of all the pieces of furniture you have in your house, you spend the most time on your bed. It only stands to reason, therefore, that investing in a quality bed will improve the overall quality of your life. But, before you commit yourself to this or that mattress, check them out. And, if you have access to the Internet, do searches of chiropractors, osteopaths, and orthopedic surgeons and see what they recommend

Now let's talk about what you should put on your bed, from the mattress surface out to the bed cover.

- Your Mattress

To start with, even if you use no mattress enhancements, most mattresses, with the exception of cotton batting futons, are made of synthetic, man made materials. We shall get to sheets and blankets in a moment. Such synthetics for the most part make your body get sweaty more easily. Some of you who have ever dozed on a mattress without sheets know how clammy you can feel as a result. Thus, it is good to get a natural, soft wool, or thick cotton under sheet that will go between your mattress and your regular sheets. You may think that this is easily or solely accomplished with the use of a mattress pad. We shall discuss these shortly.

- Mattress Enhancements

Before we do, however, there are a few mattress enhancements that can be quite helpful if you have sore joints or areas where pressure can be a bother to your rest.

The first and least expensive is an **egg-crate mattress**. Usually made of foam, these mattress toppers work by more effectively evenly distributing your weight. The result is overall less strain on any given area.

Then, there are **magnetic pads**. If you read any health or wellness magazines, you may hear about the benefits of magnetic pads for your mattress. This may sound a bit hokey, but the theory behind the ones that are of any quality is really quite sound. In 1952, a German physicist by the name of W.O. Schumann studied the electro-magnetics of the earth. He determined that the Earth has its own pulsating frequency – 7.83 Hertz – today known as the Schumann Resonance. If you were to be camping out in the woods and lying on the ground, you would be receiving this magnetic pulsating frequency that our earth is generating all the time. This is why even though the ground is pretty hard, you feel rested and your back usually doesn't bother you so much as it does at home or if you sleep on the carpet at someone else's home. In our home environments away from nature and suspended on artificial surfaces, we do not get the benefit of that magnetic resonance. So, the really good magnetic pad and mattress companies make the strength of the magnets used the exact same strength of the natural earth magnetic. And while these pads can be harder or a bit nubby where the magnets are, they can act like an egg-crate mattress by re-distributing your weight. At the same time, if this pad feels uncomfortable, it is reported by these companies that you can even place them underneath your mattress – even between the box spring and mattress and they will still be effective. This is how I chose to use one. Learn about reputable magnetic mattress companies in the **Source Appendix.**

Some of you will live in places where it can get pretty cold at night. And there's nothing quite like getting into a bed that is warm and snuggly. The simplest way to remedy this is to place any number of **microwavable pillows (listed in the Source Appendix)** or a **hot water bottle** into your bed before you get in. But, some of you will want to go with an **electric blanket.** That is fine, providing that once you have taken the chill off and warmed the bed up, that you not only TURN IT OFF, but also UNPLUG IT from the wall. Here's why.

I have counseled numbers of clients who had problems sleeping through the night. They would tell me that they would drop off to sleep, but then wake up regularly every twenty minutes or so. In almost <u>every</u> case when this condition was reported, the client had an electric blanket on their bed. And, the blanket was on a timer set for every twenty minutes on a rheostat for when the temperature goes below a certain marker. The timer or rheostat would kick on the pad switches and lo and behold, they would wake up.

Our bodies are electro-magnetic. Thus, when the electricity pulses through the coils of the pad or blanket, it is only natural to wake up. The solution is to not only turn off the blanket, but because it is well known that electricity will pulse through any electric device even when it is turned off, unplug it as well. The result? People have reported to me that as if by magic, they could sleep through the night.

So, keep your electric blanket, but as I said earlier, TURN IT OFF and UNPLUG IT.

- Mattress pads.

Often times over a mattress, one places a **mattress cover or pad.** This keeps the mattress from getting soiled over time and does add to warmth. When the mattress itself is high in plastics and other non-breathing fabrics, if one is more hot-bodied, it is easy to find oneself getting more hot and sweaty. A good quality, natural cotton fiber mattress pad is a great solution. To make it even more effective, one can still place the wool or cotton covering over the mattress between the mattress and the pad

Such mattress pads, made of natural fibers – like cotton can be hard to find. Thus if the mattress pad is also more synthetic than natural, one can likewise take a thick wool blanket or an extra fitted thick cotton sheet and place it over the mattress pad.

- And what about pillows?

Because we usually only cover our pillow with a pillowcase, it is important to find a pillow that is not too electrostatic – like many foam pillows are. They also can be quite hot to sleep on. My recommendation is to find a pillow made of down, cotton batting, or buckwheat hulls. These more easily adjust to the contours of your head and neck. In fact, when traveling, I recommend taking your own pillow to a hotel. This can make all the difference in getting a good night's rest on the road. Since everything is electro-magnetic, pillows have their own electro-magnetic charges. And, so does our heads, even our thoughts. Thus, if the person or person's before you have been having nightmares or confusing dreams or general disturbed sleep, would it not make sense that some of this vibration is something that you would pick up on? I know this is very subtle, but it is worth considering and doing something about if you can. Another thing you can do in a hotel is to take one of their towels, wrap that around the pillow and then put the case over that.

Besides your regular pillow, a nice addition to your bed comfort are one the many **herb pillows** now that use such restful herbs and flowers as linden, lavender, violet and myrrh. They are also very easy to make.

- Bed Linens and Sleep Garments

If you go to any destination spa or growing number of eco-friendly hotels worldwide, you will find plush bed furnishings; pillows, sheets, pillowcases, blankets - all made of the finest natural fibers. Why? They are indeed a bit more expensive. But, in the long run they look better and last longer, are easier to clean, and most important, they are really comfortable and help guests get great nights of rest. It's a win-win scenario. And if you get them for your own home, you will take your **first step** into creating your home spa environment!

With respect to these furnishings supporting a good night's rest, as I said earlier, we are electro-magnetic. Our body holds a charge. Think about what happens when you walk across a very synthetic carpet in your dress shoes. Have you ever then reached to turn on the lights and been shocked? Now, think about permanent press, synthetic sheets and/or pajamas made of a high percentage of nylon or acrylics. If these are what your bed linens and pajamas are made of, the electro-magnetic fields around your body builds up and you will be more agitated and restless. Another example that especially many women can attest to; i.e. when they remove their synthetic tights at the end of the day. What a relief!

The solution is choosing bed linens and sleep garments made of **natural fibers**; cotton, rayon, and silk. These will allow your body to breathe and allow your body to let go of any excessive electro-magnetic build-up. And when it comes to covers, the same applies. Choose wool or cotton blankets and down comforters. One excellent new technology for covers is far infrared blankets. These blankets are remarkable in that they help warm-bodied people cool down and cold-bodied people warm up. They have been around for about twenty years and because they last forever, they are well worth looking into. Again, sources for these blankets will be listed in the Source Appendix.

- Bed Placement

The last point about your bed is where to place it in your bedroom. There are many theories about the ideal place and direction to place your bed. Here there are two simple suggestions I encourage you to follow.

First, **don't place your bed under a window or directly against an outside wall.** These two considerations have to do with health. Even the best windows leak and cold air sinks. If your head is, therefore, below a window, there is a greater likelihood that you will catch a draft, which can be the cause of ear infections, sore throats, colds and flus. The same problem can arise from your bed being against an outside wall. Here the solution can be as simple as moving the bed a foot or more away from the wall.

The second suggestion is, **don't have your head in line with or directly opposite the doorway to the bedroom.** This has to do with our innate animal instincts and our fight-flight response. Whether we are little children or lumberjacks, we are sensitive creatures and even if in our rational mind we think we are comfortable and secure, like any animal, we are innately aware of any direction from which an unknown influence or threat can come. With our heads in front of or opposite the doorway, we tend to remain more unconsciously vigilant of our surroundings. This is great if you are a spy or soldier. But, it doesn't help anyone in need of a good night's rest.

The general atmosphere of your resting and sleeping place

- Darkness

When it comes to too much light or noise in a bedroom, the solutions are obvious, but perhaps not well understood with respect to how these two affect rest.

If you have ever been to Alaska or Scandinavia, where it is light all times of day in the summer and dark all times of day in the winter, you will notice that people there sleep very little and maybe just doze during the summer, whilst in the winter, they are like hibernating bears. Thus, if sleep is what you need, then **less light and better still, complete darkness is the prescription.** If you live in a city with bright street and sign lights around you, get good, thick blinds or curtains. And if you have to have some light in the room for some reason or another, **wear an eye mask** – one that not only covers your eyes, but also your forehead (The reason here is that your pineal gland is located here and our bones are not completely opaque. Thus, they let in light, which keeps the pineal gland stimulated.)

- Noise

With respect to noise, it's not like light. You don't have to have complete silence. In fact, if you were raised in a city, the silence of the countryside can be quite difficult to adjust to. With that said, you may enjoy relaxing music or a guided visualization CD to help you let go when you are dropping off to sleep. (Examples of music and guided relaxation CDs and companies are listed in the Source Appendix.) But, pay attention reducing as much as possible any electronic or droning sounds as much as possible. Reducing as many appliances from your sleeping environment that may cause such is advised. Just as for light, heavy curtains can shield or muffle sounds from outside. If you are hypersensitive to sounds, **earplugs** can be effective. And, from the tradition of Ayurveda, so can **a little bit of almond or sesame oil just placed into the ear canals.**

- Smell

Another sense to be aware of is smell. **Try to sleep in a well-ventilated space that does not have strong aromas, especially of food.** Like light and sound, if the sense of smell is strongly stimulated, this too, keeps the brain overly active.

- Electro-magnetic Smog

And then, there is electro-magnetic interference and smog. This is beyond the buzz or drone of appliances. Electro-magnetic smog can keep a "buzz" in a room. To reduce and clear out this intense energy, I suggest…

If you have a TV in your room, **don't fall asleep with it on.** Ideally, **turn it off at least 20 minutes before you go to bed. The same applies to a computer.**

Don't use your cell phone as your alarm clock. As it is connected to the microwave towers, it is like having a strong antenna next to your body and head. If circumstances permit, **turn your cell phone off.** And if you cannot turn off your cell phone, **put it somewhere across the room.**

If you have an **electric radio alarm clock,** these are usually very strong electro-magnetic sources. Again, don't have it very close to your body, especially your head. If you can, place it across the room (which will force you to get up on time anyway!). Alternatively, get a wind-up or battery run alarm clock.

Very often, beneath the head of the bed at the wall there will be a wall plug. Wall plugs leak a small amount of electrical current. There are any number of electrical and electro-magnetic field (EMF) shielding devices currently on the market. Electrical energy and electro-magnetic smog creates positive ions. Out in nature, the environment is charged with negative ions. Amongst the various electrical and electro-magnetic shielding devices, look into **negative ion generators.** These various items are listed in the Source Appendix.

- Temperature

Lastly, consider **turning down the thermostat to between 60 and 65 degrees** F. We are like bears. When it's colder, we want to hibernate. Too much warmth in the room or on the bed will keep you more stimulated. If you can, even **crack open the window** to get some fresh air circulating in the room. If this means putting on another cover, it will be worth it. Snuggle in and cozy down!

CHAPTER TWO

Choosing the Time to Sleep

In this chapter, we shall focus on three aspects of time. First, we shall focus on the best time to sleep. Next, how age affects sleep. Finally, as a result of age and other factors, how much rest and sleep do you need?

The Best Time to Sleep

In most cultures, we are familiar with the increments and movement of time - the seconds, minutes, hours, days, and years. We may be familiar with the concepts of centuries or millennium, but for the most part, it is in the seconds, minutes, hours, days, and years where most of us are focused. We create markers of significance in various decades – turning, twenty (We can now do whatever we want!), thirty (Oh no. Why can't I be "forever twenty-one?" And how many twenty-ninth birthdays can I have before someone notices?), fifty (This is really getting embarrassing – don't really want to talk about it at all.), or sixty (Like twenty, I feel entitled to do whatever I want or to say whatever I want to say. I've earned it!). Beyond what we can define as objective time and the cultural markers we establish regarding the significance of our age, there is the macrocosmic study of the subtle electro-magnetic affects of stars, planets, etc., commonly known as astrology, there is a micro-study of the movement of subtle energy or life force or ch'I in relation to our organ systems and the impact of such in what in Chinese medical tradition is simply called the Chinese Clock.

- The Chinese Clock

In the orient, the cultural and astrological dimensions have their own place of honor. But, what is even more interesting to me in the discussion of sleep is what is known as the Chinese Clock, paid attention to in the practice of acupuncture, but also with respect to time and timing.

The Chinese Clock breaks the hours of the day into twelve 2-hour increments. These increments of time relate to the flow of Ch'I, prana (in Ayurveda), or what we may call more generically electro-magnetic life force. This life force travels through the body in a very systematic way and its flow is identified in terms of the Five Elements or Transformations of Chinese medicine and philosophy and their related physical organ systems.

According to this theory, there is a continuous flow of electro-magnetic force coursing through us that stimulates and affects different parts of us at different times. This flow, from organ to organ, element to element is as follows...

3am-5am   – Lungs (Metal element)
5am-7am   – Large Intestine/Colon (Metal element)
7am-9am   – Stomach (Earth element)
9am-11am – Spleen/Pancreas (Earth element)
11am-1pm – Heart (Fire element)
1pm-3pm   – Small Intestine (Fire element)
3pm-5pm   – Bladder (Water element)
5pm-7pm   – Kidneys (Water element)
7pm-9pm   – Circulation-Sex Process (Fire element)
9pm-11pm – Triple Warmer (Fire element)
11pm-1am – Gall Bladder (Wood element)
1am-3am   – Liver (Wood element)

In general it is said that the hours that you sleep before midnight give you twice as much rest as those after midnight. And, the hours of darkness are the healthiest times to sleep. This is our natural sleep cycle and follows a sensibility, which is documented in scientific and esoteric traditions alike. And, in keeping with this wisdom, it is said that sleeping during the day is not advised. In both the systems of Chinese medicine and Ayurveda, it is explained that the systems of the body that need stimulation during the day become more sluggish if we sleep through the time when they should be active. Let us explore this a little more closely with respect to the above Chinese Clock schemata.

While there are probably some of you who cannot follow this next recommendation (and your concerns will be addressed shortly), **the optimal time for the average adult to get to bed is between 9 and 11pm.** This is the time of the Gall Bladder and the beginning of the stimulation of the Wood or Tree element. Before getting into the organs of the Wood element themselves, let's talk about the tissue associated with the Wood element - the muscles and connective tissue in general. The idea here is that you have been working, doing this and that all day, moving through space, demanding attention of your muscles and connective tissue. Maybe you have not been so active during the day, so you want to go out and party or go to the gym to work out some of that tension built up. That is understandable. However, some gentle stretching, maybe some yoga would be far more effective in getting this tension out than getting your system pumped and too active for the time. Rest and quietude are an important factor that needs to be considered when developing any workout, especially if you do it at night.

With respect to the organs, particularly the gall bladder and the liver, here you have the systems that are going to break down fatty substances, cleanse and rebuild your blood and replenish your muscles. To do this, the Wood element is best served **when you are lying down.**

So, what about those of you who cannot abide by this recommendation? What if you are a person works the "graveyard" shifts? Or, what if you think of yourself as a "night owl" and write or do some activity, be it writing or partying into the wee hours of the night?

The simple truth is that many such people look paler - even jaundice-ly sallow - and more stressed in general? They may have adjusted to getting up and working at midnight or built their lifestyle to be nocturnal, but the body knows better.

If your schedule or work-life demands of you this kind of schedule, here are some remedies. These can also apply to anyone who stays up during these time periods.

- During breaks, lie down. If possible, try the progressive relaxation exercise in Appendix One. If there is not enough time for this, try the technique called **speed napping**, again found in the final chapter that includes some exercises and other solutions.
- Avoid eating fatty, heavy foods during the night. If you can, stick to light fruit and vegetable dishes that are easy to digest.
- Practice the breathing exercise presented in Appendix One.

There are some exceptions to the general advice not to sleep during the day, such as for the very young or the elderly, and for persons that are weak from illness, tired from too much sex or intoxication, overwork, or emotional distress. A 10 to 20 minute catnap or progressive relaxation session can actually be helpful to recharge the body and mind if it is taken in the early afternoon. Longer naps are also sometimes advised in very hot weather between noon and three or four o'clock in the afternoon, like in the traditional 'siesta.' More will be said shortly about progressive relaxation exercises.

Looking at other time periods and sleep.

It may be of interest to note that the Chinese clock begins at 3am, the time of the Lungs. The idea here is that the first real breath of the day, the Ch'I that you will need for the day, becomes replenished in our own breath via our lungs. So, in monastic and yogic traditions around the world, practitioners get up. Catholic monks and nuns begin Vespers at 3am. Yogis think of pranayama – regulated breathing. It's an amazing time to meditate.

Yet, for the average person, the shift from the Wood element to the Metal element may only be noticed as a time to pee or one of those times when your beautiful night's sleep gets "interrupted." After all, shouldn't we get eight hours of uninterrupted sleep?

While the spiritual aspirant may look at this shift of electro-magnetics as a divine blessing, for the average person, it may feel like an intrusion. But, I contend, that it is made worse if we label this interruption as an intrusion, a sign or symptom that needs to be addressed, with therapy or medication – and more often than not, just medication.

What I would like to suggest to those who awaken at this time is to first understand what is going on and relax. When lying in bed, become aware of your breath. If you are not a meditator or yogi, just enjoy the rising and fall of your breath without judgment. This can go a long way getting you back off to sleep.

If you get back to sleep or slept through this time, probably the next "call of nature" will come between 7 and 9am. And, this literally is a call of nature. It is the time where your Large Intestine or colon is being activated. You shift around, maybe pass some gas, then you can't hold back or hold down the fort anymore. You have to go relieve yourself.

This is actually quite healthy. You may have the idea that you should not have to get up until 8 or 9am. But the fact is that this is the time of the Earth element and the stomach, spleen, pancreas, and lymphatics. It is much better to already be up and moving. With your colon clean between 5 and 7am, you are ready to meet your day.

The Ages and Stages of Our Lives – An Ayurvedic Understanding

Other than the Chinese daily clock, I mentioned earlier how age also has its own impact on sleeping. In Ayurveda, there are energetics known as doshas - Vata, Pitta, and Kapha - that are more dominant at different stages of life. Rather than get into a long description of the theory and energetics of each of these doshas, I shall just identify the time periods that they represent and how this impacts sleep. If you want more information about Ayurveda, I encourage you to look at our books referenced in the Source Appendix at the end of this booklet.

- KAPHA

From infancy to the time we are about 9 years of age, we are in what is called the **Kapha stage of life**. The Kapha stage of life shows an accentuation of the Earth and Water elements as explained earlier in my descriptions of the Chinese Clock. In this stage the physicality of our body is forming and our lymphatics are particularly active as we grow through the maturation process to the point where each system is basically functioning, as it should. This Kapha stage of life demands a lot of sleep; 10 to 12 hours a night. We start off nursing and eating and sleeping and nursing and eating and sleeping in 3-4 hour cycles day and night. Gradually, though, as our metabolic processes begin to develop and our organ systems become well established, day sleeping is replaced by naps, which then eventually dwindle to longer periods of rest at night.

This is a crucial time to trust the forces of nature and support healthy sleeping habits. Sadly, more and more parents are using media stimulation (TVs and tech devices) as baby sitters. Many "progressive" parents want to believe that their children should be able to determine when it is time to go to bed. With excess stimulation and lack of parental encouragement, more and more kids pass out in front of media, which creates its own electro-magnetic distortion. Add to this the sad tendency for manufactured treat and snack foods of children to be laden with high amounts of sugar and other additives, our lack of understanding of our Kapha/baby needs, is creating a generation more susceptible to chronic fatigue and immune compromise.

Kapha as an energetic and the Kapha stage of life **needs structure and information**. To not support children in this way and think that a laissez faire, loosey-goosey approach shows progressive thinking is to miss the boat altogether about how to encourage healthy and health-giving habits for a lifetime. So, in this stage of life, parents, show up! Get your kids to bed.

- PITTA

From the age of nine to about fifty, we are in the **Pitta stage of life**. It begins with us becoming "hormone-ized;" that is, the metabolic process with all its chemicals of transformation for shaping our bodies into the shape we shall take through our adult life. Through this transformation, hormones ebb and flow with the lunar and solar cycles of time, and the various fires (or what in Ayurveda is known as *agni*) help us to regulate our body temperature and metabolize our food.

Unlike our Kapha stage, where we are more passive than active in being responsive or reactive to our environment, here we certainly become much more as active participants in the day-to- day aspects of our lives. We have to develop our critical thinking skills and our discernment as we interact with our world. Thus along with the more physical aspects of our lives that were essential to our survival in the Kapha stage of life, our active participation, our choices and our giving into subconscious patterns has more of an impact on us. Thus, in the morass and turmoil of our teen and early adult years, sleep is not only about getting physical rest, it is also becomes vital for emotional processing. Thus it can be that – depending on what is going on around them – a teen may need hours and hours of sleep, or very little, often times dependent upon mood. If you have ever had a teenager (or can remember and/or be honest about your own teen years), you may recall that when they are bored, they can doze on and on. But, the minute a friend calls and something cool is happening, they are up like a tiger coming out of sleep to go hunt the antelope it just sniffed.

One of the hormones implicated with sleep and our bodies' rhythms is melatonin. It especially gets triggered at night in dark environments. Thus, if a TV or screen of some sort is on or the nightlights of a room are too bright, by virtue of the eyes being stimulated (the eyes being one of the "seats" of Pitta), melatonin is not activated, as it would be in a better sleeping environment. The solution, therefore, is not to buy some melatonin, but to have a more darkened, peaceful atmosphere to be in. You may recall that when I was speaking about light, I did mention the use of an eye pad that would also cover your forehead, hence your pineal gland. Deciding to flood your system with melatonin as a supplement, therefore, is an attempt to over-ride the stimulation of your sleep environment. That said, I have known of people who take melatonin when they travel by plane with good effect. But, even then, a good eye pad can be almost as helpful. In general, for this time of our life, the darker the room, the better.

In the Pitta stage of life, a combination of the water and fire elements according to Indian Ayurveda (but also including aspects of the air or metal element according to Tibetan Ayurveda), it is important to develop habits of relaxation to offset the increase of work and activity that is the hallmark of this stage of life. Being able to separate work from play, and play from relaxation; establishing a clean, comfortable sleeping environment, having good sleeping habits, avoiding excessively stimulating food or environments close to bed time, working on finding balance with respect to emotions like anger, frustration, and so forth through meditation, relaxation exercises and the many benefits of exercise regimens such as Tai Chi or the practice of yoga (especially savasana – the corpse pose) are some of the features necessary for good rest and sleep during the Pitta stage of life. Because of what life throws at us if you have a partner, kids, various responsibilities, this may be the stage of life where you get great, undisturbed sleep sometimes, then not very much at all. In this stage of life, if you have good, established habits, it will all even out. But, too often, the Pitta stage of life sees people burning the candle from both ends. If this happens over a prolonged period of time, hormones and body systems get over-taxed and stretched, the result being patterns that aggravate Vata, the next stage of life and set us up for Vata-like problems, such as insomnia. A well-known Ayurvedic physician use to tell his patients, most of whom were in the Pitta stage of their lives, that they needed to be wary of too much "hurry, worry, and curry;" being fast-paced, not resolving troublesome emotions, and indulging their senses with strong foods and beverages.

So, if you are in this stage of life, take heed! Learn to chill out and shut down. Otherwise, be aware that payback is just around the corner.

- VATA

After about fifty, until our mortal end, we are in the Vata stage of life. Known as the **wind-like dosha**, this is a combination of the tree/wood/or space element and the air/metal element in the five element schemata. We all begin to cool down and dry up. The heat of Pitta is subsiding and the metabolic processes that would burn away toxins, help us get over things with fevers, begins to subside. So, toxins stay with us longer and are harder to eliminate. Our bodies begin to slow down and do not respond as they did when we are young, but our brain – in many respects – does not age, at least in the same way. (Here we shall not address the issue of the epidemic of dementia.)

As the wind-like energy of Vata increases, our central nervous system is more and more stimulated. Our body is not moving as much and our mind is moving more. In traditional societies, this is the time of the sage, the wise person; someone who has time to rest and reflects and offers their pearls of wisdom. Sadly, in most post-industrial societies, once you hit fifty, you are just "over-the-hill." What elders think is not that important. We are not even good consumers, with the exception of medication – and one of the medications often prescribed is for sleep and insomnia. With time on our hands and being considered of little value or consequence, it stands to reason that we have difficulty sleeping.

More to the point, if we have spent a life, doing, doing, doing, we do not know how to be. We have to distract ourselves from the stillness, try to fill in the time with games and activities that only bespeak our irrelevance in everyday life.

Yet, the potential of this time lies in learning how to effectively relax and meditate; i.e. going within. Hopefully, in our Pitta stage of life, we learned about these practices. Now is the time for to master them. Thus, the problems of rest and sleep in this stage of life, I contend, have more to do with how we define and do not know how to manage this stage of life.

In this time period, because of the higher levels of stimulation to our more cerebral activity, the nature of rest and sleep changes again. We may find that we rest plenty through the day, but do not need so much complete sleep at night. After all, our body is not working as hard or at least we have less activity than when you were in your Pitta stage of life. Rather than holding ourselves to our 8-hour routine and thinking that if we do not achieve this that we are pathologically risking full system breakdown, can we learn to tap into the rhythms that come with a new stage of life?

In Ayurveda, as it is understood that this Vata stage of life comes with this heightened sense of stimulation, practitioners encourage their clients to do self-oil massage daily. Oil nourishes and calms Vata. This activity alone, called abhyanga, can go a long way in taking care of what we think of as rest and sleep problems. This process of self-abhyanga will, again, be explained in the Appendices.

In this stage of life, to calm the winds, you are encouraged to eat warmer, cooked rather than raw foods in general. You can look at our other books on Ayurvedic lifestyle mentioned in the Bibliography to get a more complete explanation as to what is most useful in diet for this stage (as well as the other stages) of life. But one of the most important things to include in your diets are healthy fats, Omega 3 fatty acids, found in a wide variety of organic, cold-pressed vegetable oils. Such oils are considered in the tradition of Ayurveda to sooth the nervous system and nourish the brain. This is different from my recommendation earlier to not eat heavy, fatty foods just before bed.

The point in mentioning these doshas or energies of Ayurveda is to point out that the various stages of our life have their own rhythms, thus needs when it comes to sleep. We need to adapt, become resilient and resourceful. If we take the needs of these energetics in combination with the understanding of the Chinese clock, follow the rules about food, napping, relaxation exercises, exercise in general and develop ways to process constricting, difficult emotions, we go a long way in preparing ourselves to live a sleep enriched life.

CHAPTER THREE

Sleep and Body, Mind, and Emotions

Now that we have looked at your bed, your room, the best times to sleep, and how to adjust your rest and sleep patterns in keeping with your stage of life, we now want to address our physical needs and habits around sleep and what I said were the most important aspects of sleep and restful sleep; your mind and emotions.

Let's start with some personal habits to get you ready for that good night's sleep...

Eating Habits

I touched upon this briefly in other sections, but it is again worth elaborating on here.

Try not to eat or drink for two hours before bedtime. This has to do with digestion. After two hours, much of your food is well on its way to being digested. Thus, in the morning, when it is breakfast time, you really will be "breaking fast." In many cases, one of the chief reasons for feeling groggy in the morning is the fact that you have been actively digesting food all night. This is making your body work when it should be resting. So, try to follow this recommendation as best you can.

That said, some of us for any number of reasons cannot get to bed without some level of warmth in our bellies. We want to snack on something. If that is you, think of something like hot herbal tea or fruit. Especially stay away from spicy or greasy foods, or caffeinated soft drinks, black tea, or coffee. For most people and in general, caffeine not only keeps you awake, but makes sleep more restless. Also, avoid alcoholic beverages before bedtime. Although a beer or glass of wine may help you get off to sleep, it often makes one rouse in the early hours and reduces the quality of rest the remainder of the night.

There may be other foods that you eat that also disturb your sleep. For some, eating fermented or cultured foods such as yoghurt or cheese (like on a pizza) right before bed can cause nightmares. In my own case, I can drink a double espresso and drop off into blissful sleep, but I am a hopeless insomniac if I eat even one small square of chocolate. So, <u>listen to your body</u>. Pay attention to and take stock of what foods help you rest and which ones make you restless all night or groggy in the morning.

Making the Transition from Daytime to Nighttime, From Work to Sleep

- **Try not to fall asleep in your daytime clothes.**

    Your daytime clothes will have the smells and feel of your daytime. Even though you are lying down, you will feel as if you are still busy with the day. Make the transition. Have bedtime clothes or pajamas that let your mind and body know that it is bedtime.

- **Wash your hands, face, and feet and clean your mouth and teeth before sleeping.**

    This is more than just for hygienic purposes. Like changing into nighttime garments, brushing your teeth and washing your face, hands, and feet is a way of shedding the oils and residues of your daytime activity. If you have never done, especially **wash your feet with warm water.** Of all these nightly ablutions, it can be the one that not only feels luxurious, but is also extremely relaxing. **If you like to shower or take a bath, don't make it too hot.** And <u>especially</u> avoid soaking your head in hot water, as this will keep your brain stimulated. Let the water get your belly and back nice and warm. This will pull circulation away from your head. Also, **avoid going to bed with wet hair.** It's a good way to catch a cold, precipitate ear problems, or a stiff neck.

Your Mind and Emotions

In the beginning of the booklet, I mentioned that the two biggest culprits in not being able to get off to sleep are a busy mind and negative emotions.

The simplest ritual to start with to calm the mind down before bed is to not get it wound up before bed! That is, don't read a scary novel, watch a gruesome crime show, troubling news just before you go to bed, or whatever grabs your emotions or gets your brain all worked up. Slow it down.

- If there is more on your mind and you know how to **meditate**, do so briefly to clear the cares and worries of the day before you close your eyes. If you do not know how to meditate, see Appendix One for some simple mindfulness-based meditations that can be done at night or any time of day. Alternatively, one can also use the **breathing exercise** recommended.

- Of course, there are times when there are some emotions that are more difficult to let go of. **Try not to go bed harboring negative emotions**. If you are living with the person you are having difficulties with, **clearing any bad feeling before going to bed** will make the atmosphere in the room much more conducive for sleep. If nothing else and if this is not possible, **don't try to force the difficult feelings away**. Sometimes accepting that they are there and just observing how they feel in your mind and body can be almost like a "counting sheep" exercise and will help you to sooth any spiky tense feelings.

- From the traditions in the east, from my own clinical practice and my own experience, an energetic technique that you can also try when your mind is fixated on one thing or another is to **rest on your right side**. According to yoga theory and the tradition of Tibetan Ayurveda, each side of the body has its own way of fueling and/or supporting various emotional states. In keeping with the explanations provide on the Channel Breathing exercise in the Appendix, the right side is associated with "attachment;" holding on to this or that state of mind, particular thoughts, and so forth. When you lie on your right side, you are actually constricting or blocking off that side, allow your mind to "let go" more easily. Test it out for yourself. That said, if what is keeping you up is a harboring of such negative emotions as anger and frustration, the left side – more associated with the negative emotions states connected to anger – may be a better choice in the beginning.

- Like the above-mentioned recommendations on which side to sleep, there are esoteric theories of which direction to lay in sleep. Most support the idea of having your head in the north from the standpoint of the earth's magnetics. Other directions can be restful or more energizing based on Feng Shui theory. For this information, a basic look at this can be found in Sally Fretwell's book, *Feng Shui: Back to Balance*. Thus, it can even be that changing directions and positions if it is at all possible to make such adaptions is helpful – and, again, a reflection in becoming more fluid and adaptable rather than getting stuck in your head about this or that direction or position being the only one that is good for you.

With all this said, I am reminded of the simple and beautiful advice of one of my beloved teachers, the Venerable Khenpo Karthar Rinpoche who demonstrated to me time and again the vastness of his wisdom. Obviously knowing that such theories and recommendations are present in Tibetan Medicine, he suggested to people that if they can imagine that their head is resting in the lap of their teacher, they will sleep peacefully. Extrapolating from his advice, in whose lap would you feel most comfortable, most at peace? Of all the variables to consider, this is probably the easiest, if not most profound.

In conclusion, along with better sleep eating habits and routines around sleep preparation, cleansing and freeing your mind of the day physically, emotionally, and spiritually is as important for a good night's rest as all the other factors combined. In Ayurveda, mind always precedes body. With the intent to cleanse and let go you have the most important tool at your disposal. Of course, this requires practice whereas all the other recommendations are about times and re-arranging stuff. So, make the adjustments where and when you can and slowly build into your life a practice that works with your mind.

CHAPTER FOUR

How much sleep do you need and what if you don't get it?

Although it is recommended that 8 hours of sleep is the general rule, please remember that this is a "general" rule. It works on average, but you may find that you need more or less than what is recommended. And this may vary considerably based on season and circumstance, and, as you have now also learned, your age and stage of life.

Like in so many other aspects of lifestyle, the wisdom from Ayurveda and other holistic healing systems considers our sleep needs to be individual. Some people tend to have light, restless sleep that is variable in quality for short periods of time (4 to 6 hours nightly). These people are generally more excitable and can easily be over-stimulated by noise, bustle of a city, an over-crowded schedule, and can, thus, easily over extend themselves. If you identify with this type of person, chances are you may need to take time for naps, relaxation, and meditation to supplement sleep. An early night after a **warm oil self-massage** as explained earlier can help calm things down and prepare you for a deep night of sleep. Alternatively, a bit of **sesame oil in a warm bath** can also work if you can't take more time. Some other warm and nurturing suggestions will be listed later on in this chapter.

Alternatively, you might be the kind of person who can drop off to sleep easily, and even though your sleep is light, you wake alert. Such people like you do best with 6 to 8 hours of sleep, but you can also manage well on very little sleep several nights in a row. If this is you, more than likely it is your hard driving nature that interferes with both the quality and quantity of your sleep. Anxiety and worldly worries that loop over and over again in your brain are the main causes for your insomnia. Along with the previous chapters recommendations on mind and emotions, taking a **cool shower, sipping a sweet (fruit, not sugared) drink,** or **going outside in**

the cool evening air to meditate in the moonlight can help to ease the worries and cool down your pent-up intensity.

Then there are people who just love to lounge, love to rest, and take life as it comes. They rarely have difficulty sleeping and enjoy long deep sleep, which lasts often longer than eight hours. Yet they awake refreshed. If this is you, then the only consideration is to **watch that you don't sleep too much**. The result of lounging about too much is that it can cause weight gain and mental heaviness. The solution that works best for you is to follow the old adage, "Early to bed and early to rise…"

We have explained that **as we get older, it is natural to find our sleep patterns changing**. We may need to rest more, but we tend to be less able to sleep for long periods of time at night. And again, rather than accept this as normal, so many people medicate themselves to try to get the same rest they needed when they were working, taking care of their families, and so on. With less physical activity and more mental activity, we simply just don't need to worry that we get up in the night. Rather than medicate, **meditate, read a book, do something that is calm, but focused for a while.** This is a normal pattern and special treatment is only needed when there is long-term exhaustion. On a personal note, I have found that I wake around 5am. In this time, I will do some yoga, meditate and then, after about an hour and a half, I go back and rest for another hour.

The bottom line is pay attention to your experience. Don't let the prescribed norms that are set by the culture or your doctor talk you into the "I have insomnia" box.

Night Time Sleep Solutions

Up until this point, we have been making general recommendations and daily lifestyle solutions for guaranteeing that you get a good night's rest. I would now like to make suggestions for more chronic sleep problems.

- Exhaustion

This may sound a bit counter-intuitive, but exhaustion can actually prevent you from getting a night's rest. There you are, you've worked hard all day. And before you get to be, there seems to be even more to do. By the time you are ready to get into bed, you are physically and emotionally spent and can barely drag your body onto the mattress. Wouldn't this seem like the perfect time to just "crash."

And, that is just the problem.

Proper rest involves stages, where our body and mind unwinds and helps us to settle into sleep. This involves our nervous system and brainwave patterns. With respect to the later, it is optimal to go from our beta wave or everyday thinking brain wave frequency through the alpha brainwave or relaxation frequency into the delta or unconscious deep rest brain waves. If we go from our normal beta waves of ordinary thinking to delta waves, i.e. just go unconscious immediately, we may not get sufficient relaxation (alpha) brainwaves to kick in. We haven't been able to put down the day. It is just a big weight on our shoulders and going to bed in this state is just about giving in – not letting go. So, we have a choppy night of sleep and wake up almost as exhausted as when we laid down several hours before.

To remedy this, do some **stretching and gentle breathing exercises**. The **Cleansing Breathing for the Subtle Channels** described in Appendix One is excellent to do at this time, as it will clear the mind. Another technique is to do the **Tibetan Rejuvenation Yoga Series** discussed in Appendix Two, which can be done in the morning to wake us up, and done at night to soothe and help us release the tensions of the day.

What you will notice from doing any of these suggestions is that you will feel more awake, but more settled in mind and body. As a result, the rest you get will be qualitatively better.

These suggestions are essential for when you are exhausted and need to sleep. But, they are also excellent for anyone as they are guaranteed to improve how deep we sleep.

- Insomnia

Many of the suggestions already made us far will go a long way to helping you if you suffer from insomnia. But here are some even more potent suggestions that you can do all together or use in combination with what I have suggested so far.

+ Oil in Ears and on Bottoms of Feet

    Take some sesame oil and lightly coat the inside of your ears. Then, take another small amount of sesame oil and lightly coat the bottoms of your feet. If you are concerned about leaving oil marks on your sheets, put some white cotton socks on. This is even cozier.

    The logic behind this comes from the tradition of Ayurveda. Oil, according to Ayurveda, especially sesame oil, can have a very calming effect. As mentioned in a previous chapter, it soothes what in Ayurveda is known as the "wind" or *Vata* energy of the body. This was discussed when I mentioned self-massage and the overall benefits of oil for our bodies. There is more information on this in Appendix One.

Oiling the ears and the feet has a calming effect on the central nervous system and will, especially if you are a light, intermittent sleeper to start with, deepen your sleep.

+ Warmth on Belly

If you ever want to help a baby get better rest and sooth its colic, just place a warm hand on the belly. Not surprising, the same can be true for us. One reason why this works is that by putting **warmth on the belly, one is attracting a greater level of circulation to the colon.** As the circulation is drawn to the colon, it becomes more stimulated while the rest of the body becomes less stimulated. To deliver continuous warmth to the belly, you can use a hot water bottle that is wrapped in a towel or any number of grain or stone filled tummy bags and warmers that have been warmed in a stove or microwave. A list of such warmers is listed in the Source Appendix. Either just before going to bed and even just after lying down, rest this warmth on your belly. And just like a baby, you will find yourself beginning to drift hypnotically into blissful sleep.

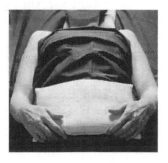

+ Rolling on Spine

This exercise can be done for insomnia or for exhaustion.

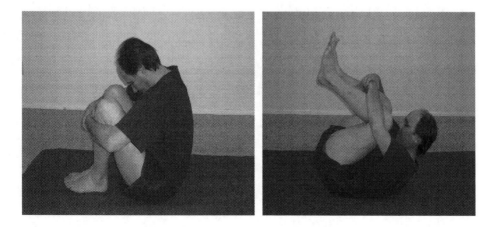

Sitting on the ground, cross your legs and hold onto your knees. Start by allowing yourself to roll backwards onto your spine. For comfort and to not damage your spine, do this on a carpet, blanket, or some kind of cushiony mat. A yoga mat is ideal.

As you roll completely back and your feet are above your head, push forward on your knees with your arms so that you get a rocking motion – back and forth on the full length of the spine. Continue to do this for about 20 to 30 times.

Often after a day where stress has gotten the better of us, we get tensed up in our shoulders or lower part of our spine. The result is an uneven distribution of circulation, hence nervous system stimulation to the entire spine. Rocking back and forth on the spine increases the circulation throughout the spine thus evens out the stimulation. Blocked or tensed areas are more easily released.

What is interesting about this technique is that when you lay down after you have done it, you will initially feel very alert. You may even wonder if you will be able to go to sleep. And then, suddenly, there you are – six to seven hours later - feeling refreshed.

+   Barefoot Shiatsu Series

This is a wonderful series as taught by the late great Shizuko Yamamoto in her classic book on shiatsu, *Barefoot Shiatsu*.

Step 1 - Abdominal massage – Lie on you back and have your legs drawn up so that the bottoms of your feet rest on the mattress and your knees are drawn up. With your fingertips rub firmly down from the top of the sternum (breastbone) continuing down the middle of your abdomen (belly) until you get to about one and a half inches below the navel. As you get into the soft part of your belly below the rib cage and chest, press deeper. Do this 4 to 5 times.

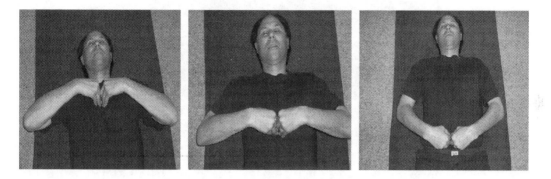

Step 2 - Starting below the navel, press down on points around the abdomen as if each point was a number on a clock. Go in a clockwise direction. Repeat 3 times pressing in as you breathe out and releasing as you let your breath in again.

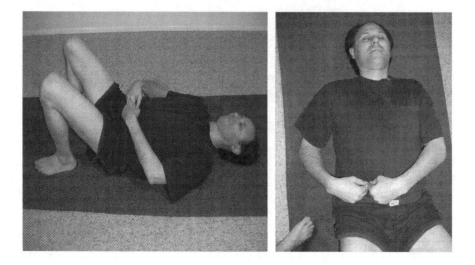

Step 3 - Use both your palms to rub your belly in a clockwise motion for about a minute.

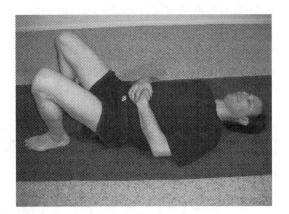

Step 4 - Leg tensing. Still lying on your back, have you legs flat on the mattress. Breathe in, tense your right leg and press the back of your right heel into the mattress while holding your breath, then relax your leg and breathe out. Do this 5 times. Repeat this with the left leg.

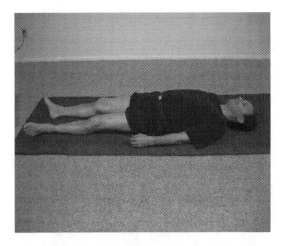

Step 5 - Upper back and neck tensing. Still on your back rest your elbows on the mattress with your arms beside your body. As you breathe in, arch your upper back and your neck so that the top of your head is on the pillow. Then breathe out and relax your back and neck. Repeat this 5 times.

Step 6 - After these 3 exercises, place your hands so that your fingers rest just below your navel. Observe your breathing – allowing your belly to rise and sink with each breath. With each breath out, imagine that you are allowing yourself to sink deeper into the mattress.

Relaxing During The Day: Skilled or Progressive Relaxation, Biofeedback, and Yoga Nidra

Regardless of how great your night's sleep was, there are some days when you need a bit of a break during the day; a time to unwind completely, recharge your batteries, then carry on. This is where skilled or progressive relaxation techniques are useful practices to be familiar with.

Spas around the world have "chill" or relaxation rooms, where clients can recline on ergonomically-enhanced lounges, smell dreamy aromatic oils, and experience blissful light or vision-scapes or listen to peace-inducing music or be prompted by guided relaxations (see Source Appendix). The goal of these various methods is to bring you out of your beta-wave brain frequency – the frequency that has to do with everyday thinking – and prompt your brains to drop down into alpha, then theta wave frequencies. Alpha, as we said early, is the restful brainwave one must have time in if one is to get a good night's sleep. Theta brain waves have to do with hypnogogic rest; that is, a creative, hypnotic state in which visions and powerful creativity can emerge. Of these two, alpha and theta, alpha is the more important. And when it comes to the science of relaxation, it I said that 20 minutes of relaxation in an alpha brainwave state is equal to getting eight hours of sleep!

Many of the relaxation enhancing products mentioned that you will find at a spa are readily available these days; ergonomic lounge chairs, essential oils, lights and DVDs and CDs of vison-scapes and relaxation music and guided exercises – all of which you will be able to find listed in the Source Appendix.

That said, the most portable of these relaxation tools is guided progressive or skilled relaxation techniques. The reason these are the most portable has to do with the fact that – in truth – the most relaxing voice you can hear is the one inside your head. Thus, once you have heard or read a relaxation exercise and get the hang of it, you talking yourself through it will be the most relaxing and effective way to get results.

Within the yoga community, there is also an increasing awareness in the benefits of deep relaxation. In general, various forms of physical yoga such as hatha or ashtanga yoga already have the concept of relaxation built into them. Although many yoga studios and their teachers are taught to move students quickly from one pose to another, this is more a fast-paced modern cultural affect than a real knowledge or practice within yoga. In actuality, the theory behind yoga teaches that the rest in between each pose allows the body to rest and integrate the experience of what one has just put the body through energetically and physically. Although this is rarely done these days, most teachers are taught to include *savasana* or "corpse" poses at the end of a yoga class to encourage such rest and integration.

But, as if to emphasize this point even more and based on the epidemic of insomnia and restlessness so many experience, the techniques of **yoga nidra** are being introduced and many teachers are learning to lead entire classes in this yoga of "sleep," which is in fact what *nidra* means. More than likely, many of the progressive or skilled relaxation techniques employed today have their root in this branch of yoga. However, the progression through the body that yoga nidra leads its participants through may well indeed be more skillful and therapeutic. And, like progressive relaxation techniques, one can learn to practice them on ones own, perhaps with the aid of a CD or DVD at first, but eventually in hearing one's own voice skillfully lead the way into deep rest.

As stated earlier, the purpose of the various forms of skilled relaxation is to help a person to experience a change in brainwave patterns; moving from the beta frequency or everyday discursive brainwaves to *alpha* frequency, the brainwaves that facilitate deep relaxation. To accomplish this, the most effective of these techniques primarily focus on body sensation and/or breathing patterns. While I think it is great to look for a yoga nidra class or someone who is versed in leading others through progressive relaxation or biofeedback techniques, you will find an excellent relaxation process in Appendix One as well as a listing of such and places to get them in the Source Appendix.

No matter what kind of relaxation exercise you learn to practice, realize that it <u>is</u> a skill. For rather than sleep, where you hope you will just drop off at some point, relaxation exercises are about progressively taking yourself to that place where you begin to get that "floaty," alpha brainwave feeling, stay in it, then bring yourself back up into everyday awareness. In the beginning of learning such practices, it is advised that you **try them at home first**, so that you don't find yourself snoozing at work! And if you are home, **don't do relaxation exercises in bed.** This may sound strange, but it has to do with the fact that we are animals of habit. Lying on your bed, more than likely you will go beta, mattress, snooze…! Lie on a couch, on some blankets on the ground, or even sit in a lounge or comfy chair.

If You've Missed a Night's Sleep

I once saw a cartoon that read, "I normally try to take one day at a time. But lately, several of them have been ganging up on me all at once."

There are times due to travel and other events in our lives, that we need more than 24 hours to complete the day or there simply has not been the time to really put down the time. Feeling cheated and wanting to make up for it, we think that all we need to do is sleep it off during the day and we'll be right as rain. I ask you, has this ever worked? For example, with jetlag, it often takes several days to acclimate. We still feel woozy until we have adjusted. Similarly, if it is not jetlag but some other reason, just sleeping the next day does not usually get us back on kilter.

The Tibetan tradition of Ayurveda offers a formula to help us through this time more effectively. This recommendation is made, taking into consideration that insomnia is something different and needs to be handled per recommendations made earlier.

According to the Gyud Zhi, the medical texts of Tibetan Ayurveda, if you cannot get sleep per your normal routine, in the morning time, avoid breakfast, and then try to sleep at once or in increments during the day of what would amount to one-half of your normal sleep. That is, if you normally sleep eight hours at night, try to get four hours of sleep during the day. The reason you do not eat breakfast is that with your belly filled and your digestive process engaged, you will not be able to rest as deeply or get as much benefit from your rest as your body is still working. Of course, if you are hungry for something, take a light snack based on the suggestions I have provided earlier. The idea here is not to make up entirely for the night of sleep missed, but to get your body more relaxed, thus the Vata dosha or energetic calmed down sufficiently to support you getting a much better start to your subsequent night's sleep.

Speed Napping

While skilled or progressive relaxations usually takes a minimum of 20 minutes, here is an exercise that can give you a great quality of rest in just minutes. It comes from the Taoist tradition. Based on using the subtle energy acupuncture meridian system, it is a technique that relies specifically on body position and doesn't require any particular focus or thought process whatsoever. Assume the position, let go and in less than ten minutes, you are supercharged and can get on with your day! It really is magical and is so versatile technique that you can do it behind your desk, in your break room, - literally wherever you can sit back on a chair or couch. You can even do this at home. But, again, don't perform this on your bed. Again – bed equals sleep.

STEP ONE: Assume the following posture. Either lying down or sitting up, wrap your right hand fingers around your thumb and place this fist over the area of the heart. Then wrap your left fingers around your left thumb and place this fist a bout 1.5 inches below your navel. If on a chair with no arms or table, you may need to place pillows or bolsters under the arms to keep your fists over these areas. Next, cross your right leg from the ankle down over your left leg.

STEP TWO: Rest your tongue behind your top front teeth, close your eyes and let your head drop. Let go entirely. Allow yourself to feel like your letting yourself go to sleep.

Within 7 to 10 minutes you will naturally wake up, alert and refreshed. 'Why?' you may ask – which of course is not a proper question when examining oriental traditions. The issue here is 'how?' Simply put, the position you assumed for this exercise seals the subtle body energy so it does not dissipate. At the same time, it allows the natural charge of Ch'I or life force to stream in. Within 10 minutes, you're topped up and ready to go.

Simple Medicinal Approaches

If after trying all of these lifestyle adjustments and remedies you still find that you are not getting proper sleep, consult your physician or health care practitioner. Rather than expecting them to prescribe a tranquilizer, ask them to check your **calcium, potassium, and B vitamin levels.** Just a few natural supplements may be just the boost you need to relax your body and get that needed rest. And to be honest, I would suggest that you go to them first before heading to the natural food store and consulting with the person who runs the supplement section.

Along these lines, a good friend and psychiatrist by the name of Dr. Florian Birkmeyer has created a formulation based upon his years of study of Aromatherapy and the clinical; application of essential oils and hydrosols. I present this here with his full permission.

Dr. Birkmeyer's Sleep Oil

Blend spikenard (Nardostachys jatamansi) essential oil and cardamom essential oil in a ratio of 3:1 in a carrier oil. I often use apricot kernel oil as a carrier because it is light and easy to apply. In terms of concentration, I find 18 drops of spikenard and 9 drops of cardamom in 5ml quite sufficient.

To use it: I recommend anointing yourself and you set an intention for a night of restful sleep. An easy way to anoint is what I call the '9-Point Anoint'.
Simply dab half a drop on each of the following points in this order:

1. the right temple
2. third eye area (center of the forehead)
3. left temple
4. the right jugular area (or more precisely a point 2 fingers below the mastoid process)
5. the area between upper lip and nose
6. the left jugular area
7. the right wrist pulse point
8. the heart area (midpoint of the sternum)
9. the left wrist pulse point.

Remember not to fight or resist the wave of relaxation that will set it soon.

Re-writing the fretful "I can't sleep" Story

So, we get off to sleep sort of OK, but then wake up in the early ours. And we fret. We just can't leave it alone. Not understanding nature's times and cycles of which we are a biological part, we get the idea in our heads that we need to do something about this. So, we start taking over-the-counter or prescription sleeping medication. Invariably, all of these medications tend to make us constipated. Thus, we may sleep, but the natural urge to defecate is inhibited and blocked. We become more toxic, which interferes with the other organs, we become more tired, and the cycle escalates.

In my own case, I have chosen to re-write my 3am story. In my own mind I consider that God, the Buddhas, or other divine spirits are inviting me to sit quietly, to pray, to breath, to appreciate life. And, if I meet this time in this way, within twenty minutes or so I am back on my pillow and actually getting better rest than I would have had I just drifted along or worst still, fretted.

There is also an alternative to this positive, or uplifting approach that was shared with me from a fellow therapist who has been the student of the works of the modern father of hypnotherapy, Dr. Milton Erikson. It is such an interesting and counter-intuitive approach that I feel it bears mentioning. This comes more of as anecdotal suggestion.

What Dr. Erikson suggested was, that when you unwillingly wake up in the night, do NOT do anything useful. In fact, do something that you hate; something that is boring, tedious – something you have been putting off. Maybe it's waxing the floor, doing your taxes, repairing some complicated knickknack. After doing this, stay up the rest of the night. You'll be exhausted all the next day. Then, when it's time to go to bed, go to bed. And, Dr. Erikson claims, you'll sleep through the night from that point on. In this approach, I believe that what is happening that as a result of disliking what you did, you will have sent a subliminal message to your subconscious that you don't want to go through another night like that!

I have never done this, because I have never had to. But, if you have tried all else, perhaps this is an approach you might want to consider.

CONCLUSION

In this little booklet, I have attempted to give you skills and ways of thinking on how to achieve quality rest, relaxation, and blissful sleep. What I have offered is not exhaustive, so beyond what I suggest here, there may be more you wish to explore and experiment with. With the exception of Dr. Birkmeyer's aromatherapy sleep remedy, I have specifically avoided recommendations of any herbs formulas, teas, or specific medicines because when you are playing with biochemistry, there is so much variation that you really do need the skill of a very well trained herbalist, homeopath, and/or holistically aware or sensitive physician or pharmacologist to really understand what would work best for you. At the same time, I have seen that the approach I offer here has proven helpful to many, thus am happy to present it here without these more clinical dimensions. And, in the spirit of KISS (Keep It Simple Stupid), my recommendation to you is to start with just a few changes and add other dimensions to create your own rest and sleep environment and habits. Trust your intuition and start first with what you would find enjoyable to change and/or add.

On average, each of us needs one-third of each day devoted to quality rest and sleep. As we learn the skills to take care of ourselves, we contribute to new levels of wellbeing that benefit our body, mind, and spirit. We then learn that we are at our best not when we are revved up on coffee or living on our adrenaline, but when our minds and body are supple and relaxed. Living a more balanced, vitality-supporting lifestyle, getting our "beauty sleep" and knowing how to put down the day with skilled relaxation and meditation are not luxuries. They are indispensible features of an enjoyable and fulfilling life. And the king or queen of rest and relaxation IS sleep. That is why the best way get your day started is a Good Night's Sleep.

If you re-defined your day as beginning in the evening with the beauty of a good night's sleep, how would this change your awareness and attitude towards your daily activities?

Don't answer me here. Just sleep on it.

APPENDIX ONE

#1 Guided Visualization – A Progressive Relaxation Exercise

This exercise is designed to be read to you. Or, you can record it so that you get use to your own voice and rhythm.

"The following relaxation exercise is to begun lying flat on the ground with your knees drawn up, your feet resting on the ground, your hands palms down resting about an inch below either side of your navel, your fingertips almost touching. Allow your eyes to gently close, the tip of your tongue resting behind your top front teeth so that your jaw is loose and your back teeth are not touching.

Become aware of your breathing…..the breath coming in and out at your nostrils…..becoming deeper and deeper. Notice the rising and sinking of your belly beneath your palms and fingertips as you breathe.

What now follows are a series of breathing techniques. Each technique will involve counting the breath in and counting the breath out in a particular rhythm. You want to breathe in…..out…..or hold for the time that I am counting. The breath should always come in and out through your nostrils.

Let us begin with the first technique…..During this technique you will be inhaling to the count of four and exhaling to the count of four. As you breathe in, try to be aware of allowing your belly to gently rise, paying attention to how your body feels…..As you breathe out, allow the belly to settle and feel as though you are completely letting go. The outbreath is the breath that allows you to feel that relaxation is spreading through your entire body.

At this time, take a short breath in…..and out…..and let us begin.

INHALE 2 3 4 and EXHALE 2 3 4

INHALE 2 3 4 EXHALE 2 3 4

(Repeat 7 more time for a total of 9 repetitions.)

…..and let your breathing come back to normal as you pay attention to the different sensations moving through your body…..*(about 30 seconds)*

The next breathing technique will involve a little more concentration…..When I say INHALE, allow yourself to take a full deep breath in to the count of 6. When you have as much air as you can take in, hold your breath for a moment and tighten all the muscles of your belly, buttocks, and genital region. Contract and tighten all of these muscles and then - at the same time - EXHALE to the count of 6, keeping these muscles contracted the entire time – like you are squeezing all of the air out of your body. When all of the air is out, keep holding all of these muscles tight and DO NOT allow any breath to come in for the count of 6. After the count of 6, let go of all the muscles and take a deep breath in to the count of 6. Then, repeat as before – tightening all of the muscles mentioned and exhaling - holding the muscles tight when all of the breath is out - then releasing the muscles and inhaling again…..We'll do this 9 times…..

So take a short breath in…..then out…..and let us begin…..

(!) INHALE 2 3 4 5 6 and

CONTRACT your belly muscles and groin and

EXHALE 2 3 4 5 6 and

HOLD the breath out – hold the contraction 3 4 5 6

and release all of your muscles and

(2) INHALE 2 3 4 5 6

and tighten up and EXHALE 2 3 4 5 6 and hold the breath out and contraction 3 4 5 6 and release and

(3) INHALE 2 3 4 5 6

Tighten up and EXHALE 2 3 4 5 6 and hold the breath out and contraction 3 4 5 6 and release and

(4) INHALE 2 3 4 5 6

Tighten up and EXHALE 2 3 4 5 6 and hold the breath out and contraction 3 4 5 6 and release and

(5) INHALE 2 3 4 5 6

Tighten up and EXHALE 2 3 4 5 6 and hold the breath out and contraction 3 4 5 6 and release and

(6) INHALE 2 3 4 5 6

Tighten up and EXHALE 2 3 4 5 6 and hold the breath out and contraction 3 4 5 6 and release and

(7) INHALE 2 3 4 5 6

Tighten up and EXHALE 2 3 4 5 6 and hold the breath out and contraction 3 4 5 6 and release and

(8) INHALE 2 3 4 5 6

Tighten up and EXHALE 2 3 4 5 6 and hold the breath out and contraction 3 4 5 6 and release and

(9) INHALE 2 3 4 5 6

Tighten up and EXHALE 2 3 4 5 6 and hold the breath out and contraction 3 4 5 6 and release and

Release the muscles, allowing your breath to come back to normal…..Allow your legs to come down now so you are lying totally flat and your hands are beside your body with your palms up.

Keep your breathing calm and regular, paying attention to the different sensations moving through your body as you allow yourself to become aware of the contact your entire body has with the ground…..your heels…..the backs of your legs…..your buttocks…..your back…..all the way up to your shoulders…..your arms…..the back of your head…..

Settle into comfort and release even further.

(Allow your body to stay like this for 2 minutes)

Now, slowly, but in your own time, begin to move your fingers…..your toes…..allow your head to move from side to side…..and as you take a deep breath in, allow yourself to fully stretch…..open your eyes, and move into your day…..

#2 BREATHING EXERCISE for developing awareness of and cleansing the subtle channels…

This technique was taught to me by Dr. Lobsang Rapgay, a Tibetan physician and Ph.D. teacher and clinician at UCLA. It is rooted in an understanding of Ayurveda and chakra system used in yoga and most of the meditative traditions of the East.

The subtle channels called the 2 NADIS and central channel (Shushumna) begin about 4 finger widths below the navel. The right or RED channel, representative of the female energy (i.e. menstrual blood) starts here, moves at a distance of one "tsun" (about .75 inches) from the right side of the spine (neither to the front or back, but deep within). It passes through the neck, over the brain, but underneath the skull bones, drops down from the right side of the Crown Point, ending at the outside tip of the right nostril. The WHITE channel, representative of male energy (i.e. semen) mirrors the RED channel pathway on the left side. Although these two channels wrap and bind the central channel at various points to form what we call the chakras, in this exercise we visualize them as straight, tinted, but transparent hollow tubes, the thickness of our little finger. The Central (also called spiritual, neither male, nor female) channel is visualized as a straight tube that is two little finger widths in diameter. It is often visualized as of a yellow tint, but in this exercise we see it as a transparent blue tube that starts 4 finger widths below the navel and goes up through the body anteriorly to the spine. It goes through the neck and head to the Crown Point where it makes a tight turn downwards to the area of the "third eye" and hooks inwards (or posteriorly) towards the pineal gland.

As mentioned, the RED and WHITE channels are wrapped around the Central Channel forming constrictive knot, known as chakras. The purpose of Tantric practice is to release the pressure of these outer channels so that energy moves freely through the Central Channel. The number of chakras there are varies in accordance with the mastery of the adept. As one becomes more aware of subtleties, the number of chakras can be as many as 9.

The practice:

1. Visualize that the beginning of the WHITE channel inserts into the beginning of the RED channel below the navel. (The RED tube opening is seen as larger and capable of accepting the smaller WHITE tube end.)
2. Block your right nostril with your right index finger and inhale through your left nostril. Imagine that the air you are breathing in to your left nostril is pure and fresh and that this pure and fresh air is being carried through the WHITE channel to where the WHITE channel is inserted into the RED channel below the navel.
3. At the point where you are visualizing that the pure, fresh air is at the beginning of the RED, let go of the right nostril and with your left index finger, block the left nostril. As you exhale, visualize that the pure, fresh air is pushing out what is unclean, contaminated, polluted, like wind that blows away dust. Especially see that as you breathe out you are releasing the defilement or poison of ATTACHMENT or clinging. These negativities are seen as smoke leaving the right nostril.
4. Repeat this two more times. After this, allow yourself to breathe through both nostrils and visualize the right, RED, channel as being luminous and purified of all negativities.
5. Now repeat 1 through 4 for the cleansing of the WHITE channel. See the RED channel end fitting inside the end of the WHITE tube end. Start with blocking the left nostril. As the fresh, pure air goes from the RED channel into the WHITE channel, you breathe out the impurities and the defilement of AGGRESSION. Do this three times and then breathe in and out normally a few times, seeing the WHITE channel now as luminous and pure.
6. Now visualize Shushumna, the Central, and spiritual, Channel. It is blue and the thickness of 2 small finger widths. Visualize that both the end of the WHITE and RED channels are inserted into the end of the Central Channel. Once you see this in your mind's eye, place your hands in your lap. Allow the back of the right hand to rest in the palm of the upturned left hand. The thumbs then touch to form a triangle. With your hands in this configuration, raise them enough to make it so that your navel is in the center of this triangle.

7. Breathe in through both nostrils so that the pure, fresh air goes up through the nostrils, down through the RED and WHITE channels to the bottom entrance to the Central Channel.

8. As you exhale, feel this pure air cleansing the Central Channel and with it the defilement of IGNORANCE. You visualize that IGNORANCE and all of the impurities are pouring out of the region of your third eye.

9. Repeat this two more times. Then lower the hands into the lap and breath normally, experiencing the Central Channel as luminously blue, supple, and purified.

#3 Self-Abhyanga

Abhyanga means "Loving Hands." It is full body oil massage. Self-abhyanga is recommended in Ayurveda. As we get older, to nourish the skin and relax the body, one can do this every day. If done early in the morning, you will feel light and relaxed all day. If done in the early evening, it will prepare you for a quiet, blissful night of sleep.

What follows is a simple sequence that you can offer beneficial results.

You will be focusing on delivering the oil evenly over your entire body, giving an extra focus to large muscle areas, joints, and special energy points (or *marmas*).

What You Will Need:

+ Quality organic massage oil – sesame or sunflower based if available
+ 2 sheets; one for the ground and one for covering you that can both get oily
+ a couple towels that you don't mind getting oily
+ A powder known as an ubtan. The simplest form of ubtan is plain chickpea (garbanzo) flour, known in India as *besan* flour. Used at the end of the massage it will ensure that you feel light and relaxed rather than heavy.

Procedure:

1. Set out a sheet so that you can stand, kneel, and lie on it. Fold it in half lengthwise you it will absorb oil and won't mess up the floor or carpet. Have the extra sheet, the towels, and all other supplies close by or on the sheet.

2. Remove all your clothes and any jewelry that will get in the way.
   Using the massage oil, follow the sequence…

3. Scalp – Spread the oil through your scalp and then use your fingertips and scrub back and forth vigorously. Afterwards, following the direction of the subtle energy, stroke your hands over your head, starting at your forehead and moving back over the skull. Then find, 3 marma points, one at the CROWN, one at the anterior fontanel, then the posterior fontanel. (These are points 1,2, and 3 on the photo.) Light press and massage with clockwise circular strokes each point in the above sequence.

4. Ears - Massage along the outer edge (pinna) of your ears, from top to bottom. Pull on your earlobes, then rub the ears back and forth.
5. Face – Starting at your chin, spread the oil up over your entire face. Rub the cheeks vigorously, especially along your jaw joint. Then rub back and forth across your forehead. Place your three middle fingers on each temple, another powerful vital energy point (marma). Close your eyes and just for a moment, think of a beautiful place that makes you think of peace and relaxation.
6. Neck – With long strokes, let your fingertips put oil on either side of your throat. Stroke from below your chin down to the top of your sternum. Do this several times. This improves the circulation to your complexion. Then stroke along the side and back of your neck, from the top down.
7. Shoulders – Starting with the right shoulder, rub down from the neck, then vigorously over the shoulder joint (where the shoulder meets the arm). Repeat on the left side.
8. Chest – from the base of the ribs and sternum, bring oil up along the right side of the sternum, over the breast and then down the right side. Do this 5 to 7 times, like in a

continuous circle. Repeat this on the left side. Find the vital energy point in the center of the sternum (*hridayam*), and do light clockwise circles on this point.

9. Abdomen – Lie on your back with your knees drawn up. Apply the oil in clockwise circles around the abdomen. Using both hands, alternate going light them deeply around and around the entire abdomen, from below the rib cage to the top of the pubis). Do this for a minimum of 3 minutes. Then placing both of your hands on the area just below the navel, breathe in and out deeply for at least a minute. With each breath, feel your belly rise and with each breath out, feel like your back is just sinking and settling more relaxed onto the ground.

10. Arms - Staring with the Right arm, massage each finger joint with oil. Rub along the back of the hand, then smooth out the thick pads on the palm. With your left hand's fingers, make a band around your right wrist and rotate your right arm so that you are getting a good rubbing (like an old-fashioned Indian robe burn) around the wrist.) Then rub oil up along the forearm. Rub vigorously around the elbow joint. Squeeze up along the muscles of the biceps and triceps. Finally, place your left thumb in the deepest part of your right armpit. Press gently in and massage this marma point with clockwise rotating motions. Do this for a few moments. Rest a moment. Then, repeat on Left Side.

11. Legs – Sitting with your legs in front of you, start with the right foot. Massage and rotate each toe, starting with the big toe. Rub between the bones on the top of the foot. Rub the bottom of the foot back and forth. Rub all over the ankle joint and slowly move up the calf to the knee. Squeeze up along the calf muscles. Rub vigorously all around the knee. Then, work your hands up over the upper leg muscles to the hip joint. Repeat this on the left leg.

12. Buttocks and Genital Region – Much stress and tension is carried in this area. At first you may feel uncomfortable touching yourself in these areas. But, with time, you'll see the benefits ease in movement, improved libido and sexual performance. FOR MEN: Oil between the space between the back of your scrotum and the front of your anus. Rub back and forth in this crease between your legs. Apply thumb pressure up into this space to benefit the prostate. FOR WOMEN: Oil the area behind the back of the vagina and the front of the anus. Press up and massage into this area.

13. FOR BOTH: With your oil, apply deep, circular motions with your fists or palms of your hands to your buttocks. Do both at once in alternating fashion. As they are large, strong muscles, apply the circular motion for 25 to 35 times.

14. Back – Apply oil to the lower back as high up as you can get. Do the same from the back of the shoulders down. Rub up and down along both sides of the spine as best you can.

To get additional stimulation to the rest of the spine, lay on your back with your legs curled up. Rock back and forth on your spine for 25 to 35 times as was described in the exercises to overcome insomnia.

15. Cover your body with a sheet and rest quietly for about 3 to 5 minutes. Allow the oil to penetrate for a few more moments as you rest.
16. Take about ½ cup of ubtan powder and sprinkle it like baby powder, starting at your head, then a light dusting over the entire body. Make sure you are entirely covered, from head to toe.
17. Rap yourself up again and rest for another 2 to 3 minutes.
18. Get up, drink a glass of room temperature water, and then shower.

#4 Shamatha or Calm Abiding Meditation

The purpose of Calm Abiding Meditation is to calm and clear the mind, and bring us into a state of equanimity. Our minds are like agitated pools of muddy water. If we learn how to calm the agitation, the mud settles to the bottom and the water become clear and fresh. The methods of *shamatha* are techniques to calm the agitation. With the mud settled, we can taste the water and appreciate it for what it us. Wholesome and satisfying. Appreciation and a greater sense of aliveness arise naturally – as it was always there. But, in our restless, distracted state, we could not see or appreciate this. And, like the clear quality of a still pool, we begin to see things clearly, without distortion.

Shamatha or Calm Abiding Meditation has been around for thousands of years and is used in both religious and secular cultures. It is both simple and profound. The best results are gained if one practices it regularly; in a quiet place, at a regular time, for approximately 20 minutes. The main emphasis in the technique is resting your mind on the natural movement of the breath.

STEPS in the Meditation

1. Sit in a comfortable position. If you can sit comfortably on the ground with your legs crossed, place yourself of a semi-firm cushion that is roughly six inches high, so that the lumbar curve of your spine is natural. Full lotus is optimal, but not necessary. What is important is that your knees are below the level of your navel. If they are that high or higher, sit on a higher cushion. Your knees below your navel will allow your diaphragm to relax and make your breathing more natural. If you need to sit on a chair, try to sit

forward so that your back is away from the back of the chair. Whether on the ground or in a chair, allow your hands to be palms down on your knees.

2. To make your spine as straight as it can be, press down with your palms on your knees to straight your arms, giving the spine a lift. Then, relax the arms.

3. Your chin should be slightly tucked so that your head is not tilted back nor cocked forward. Your tongue should rest just behind your top front teeth, at the place where you would begin to say the word, "cluck." Allow your lips to be relaxed, even a bit parted.

4. Your eyes should be slightly open with your gaze towards the ground along the line of your nose. This is about 18-24 inches before you if you are on the ground. If you are in a chair, place your little fingers on your knees and open your hands so that your palms are standing up. Draw an imaginary line between your thumbs and bisect that line with the gaze of your eyes. Do NOT stare. Just allow the eyes to be partially or gently open, the focus relaxed. To make it less intense and more general, imagine the point about an inch above that line of focus.

5. Your breath is going in and out naturally from your nostrils.

6. Breathe in through your nostrils and tense your abdomen and groin, and anus. Hold the breath for a few seconds, then release the tension and your breath so that you feel as if you are sitting even more firmly on your seat. Become aware of allowing your belly to soften so tat it rise and sinks naturally with each breath.

7. Focus the attention on your breath at your nostrils. Then, as you breathe in, you follow it all the way to your abdomen as it expands naturally. As you breathe out, note the breath rising and leaving at the tip of your nostrils. Focus particularly on this sensation and get a sense of the air moving from your nostrils towards the area where your eyes are gently focused. Imagine that that is where your air simply dissolves.

8. The first part of the meditation is actually a concentration exercise. Let the breath go in and out and as it does, ascribe a number to each outbreath. The breath comes in and as it goes out and dissolves into the space in front of you, you mentally say, "ONE." The next breath comes in and as it goes out, you think, "TWO." Do this to twenty-one. If your mind wanders from the counting and you lose track, just say to yourself the word, "thinking," and go back to "ONE" and start the count again.

9. Once you have successfully counted to twenty-one, allow your mind to rest on your natural breath, most particularly your outbreath. Again, if your mind wanders from your attention on your natural outbreath, just say to yourself the word, "thinking," and go back to your breath. It does not matter what you are thinking. Just let go of your fixation on whatever the thought is and rest your mind on the breath.

10. Give yourself twenty minutes to do this meditation. If this seems to long for you, start with five minutes and work your way up to twenty. You may then expand the time to forty minutes, then an hour. The important point is to be consistent with your meditation practice. Short periods done regularly will yield better results than long periods done randomly.

The goal of such meditation is to naturally feel the integration of mind and body, which will allow the sense of equanimity to naturally arise. One learns to give up fixation on various thoughts and feelings by experiencing how they come and go, as does the breath. As we come to see that this is true in our own lives, we can also see how this happens for others – how distraction and various forms of torment or suffering go hand in hand.

Practicing to develop calm and equanimity helps us to see others and our world in a whole new way. We get in touch with a sense of wholesomeness of our natural being. And in deepening this experience through ongoing practice, compassion and genuine caring for others arises effortlessly.

APPENDIX TWO

Tibetan Rejuvenation Exercises

From the Tibetan Ayurvedic tradition, there are series of five exercises that slow the aging process and can actually help to reverse the aging process. In both the first and second editions of my book, *Tibetan Ayurveda*, I call these Tibetan Rejuvenation Exercises. A simple form of yoga that was taught in Tibetan monasteries and retreats, serious meditators, monks and nuns performed them, not because they wanted to look young and beautiful, but because they helped them maintain a suppleness in mind and body that would allow them to engage in their spiritual practices with greater focus and clarity for as long as they were alive.

If practiced in the morning, Tibetan Rejuvenation Exercises will get the body and mind up and ready to face the day. If done at the end of the day, even before bedtime, they help to relax one and smooth out the stresses and strains of the day. They actually improve the quality of your sleep. If done before meditation or prayer, they will facilitate a deepening of your experience.

As they are based on very standard yoga postures, they are also an excellent introduction for those who may wish to sample what yoga can do for them. And, it is my experience as a yoga instructor that I have never seen series of yogasanas as succinct deliver as many benefits. What is also nice is that each of the exercises can be modified to suit older and infirmed guests and still create wonderful results.

Exercise #1

We start with spinning, like the whirling Dervish tradition of Sufism. In this context, the spinning activates the chakra/endocrine systems. It also activates our vestibular system, engaging our brain and nervous systems. The physical stimulation and energy activated by the spinning makes all of the other exercises of this series beneficial.

It is natural for a person to feel some level of dizziness from doing the spinning. That is the sign of a healthy vestibular system. Thus, do not be alarmed. Also, as with all of these exercises, start slow. Begin with 7 spins and gradually work up to 21. For those who feel too dizzy or nauseous, before starting to spin, focus on a point in front of you. Make it so that as you complete each spin, your eyes return to the same point. This is what ballerinas and other performers who are required to spin do if need be.

Stand straight and allow your arms to be outstretched with fingers extended, palms downward. Keep your arms at shoulder height; not above, not below. Rest your tongue on the roof of your mouth, just behind your teeth. At a physical level, this allows for a freer flow of cerebro-spinal fluid to move along your spine. In turn, at a more subtle level, it activates a *marma* or vital energy point, known in Sanskrit as *Brahma-Randra*, the crown point of the skull. This allows more psychic and spiritual energy to enter the body. And where the tongue is touching is an important Taoist point that connects the Brain Governor and Conception Vessel, the two primary meridians of the body, creating a powerful flow throughout the body. Keep this tongue position for all of the exercises.

Spin in a clockwise direction. This means that your right arm drops back as your left arm moves forward. Spin at a comfortable rate.

At the end of the number of spins, place your hands on your hips. Breathe in through your nose and out through your mouth two to three times. Then lie down on a carpet or mat with your arms to your sides, palms down. The palm-down position of the hands also seems to lessen the dizzy feeling. Allow your breath to return to a normal, even pace. Observe your body sensations as you rest. As in the performance of any yoga program the rest between exercises is important.

Exercise #2

On your back with your arms to your sides and the palms downward, you inhale whilst simultaneously bringing your head off of the ground so that your chin comes towards your chest and raising your straight legs so that they come perpendicular to the ground. A little beyond perpendicular is fine, but try to keep the legs as straight as possible. Then, exhale and lower your head and legs to the ground, again simultaneously. Allow all of your muscles to relax for a moment and, then, repeat the exercise. Work up to 21 repetitions.

There are modifications you can make to this if you have injuries or weak abdominal muscles. If there are low back problems, tuck your hands, palms down, under the small of your spine. If there is still too much strain, bend the knees to the degree that helps. Over time, through repetition, you may find that your back and abdominal muscles will become strong enough to perform this exercise with straight legs. **The tradition of yoga teaches that you should visualize in your mind's eye that you are performing the exercise perfectly. Body follows mind, thus you may find that your back and abdomen become stronger to perform this or any of the other exercises without modifications. <u>This advice is applicable to all forms of exercise.</u>**

All of the Rejuvenation Exercises that follow the initial spinning emphasize stretching and bending the spine. Yoga teaches that in order to stay youthful and to rejuvenate, we need to maintain flexibility in the spine. In Exercise #2 you are working the sacral and occipital pumps while stretching the cervical and lumbar spine. This allows for more efficient cerebro-spinal fluid movement through the entire spine. This benefits the entire nervous system and encourages proper circulation in all internal organs.

At the completion of however many repetitions that you do, lie quietly, allowing your breath to return to normal, observing body sensations.

Exercise #3

Position yourself now so that you are in a kneeling position, your knees about one fist distance apart and your toes curled up. Your torso is straight and in line with your upper legs. Allow your hands to rest or clasp just below the buttocks on the back of the thighs, or on the buttocks themselves. Place your chin on your chest.

As you inhale, lift and draw back your head back as far as it will go whilst you lift your chest and throw open your shoulders so that your upper spine is arched. Do not lean back. Then, as you exhale, return the chest and shoulders to a more natural position and allow your chin to once again rest on your chest. Repeat this as many times as you feel comfortable up to 21. Once you are finished, sit back on your legs or any way in which you feel comfortable. Close your eyes, settle your breath, and observe body sensations.

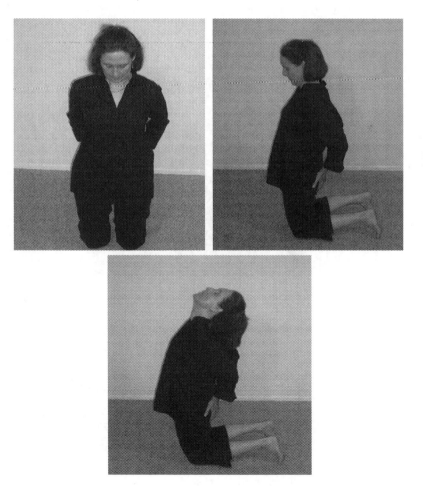

This activates the thyroid, parathyroid, thymus the energy vortices/chakras of the neck and chest. It also stimulates the brachial plexus at the base of the neck, strengthening the arms, shoulders, and increasing circulation to the lungs, heart, and chest region in general.

Exercise #4

Sit so that your legs are before you, outstretched, and your feet are about twelve inches to a shoulder width apart. Place your arms to your sides so that your hands are palms down on the ground beside your buttocks, your fingers pointing towards your feet. (If your arms are shorter or longer than to feel comfortable directly beside your torso, you may need to adjust your arms so that your hands are resting slightly behind or in front of the line of your torso. As you do the entire exercise, experiment to see where they seem best positioned.) Your chin rests on top of your sternum, as in Exercise #3.

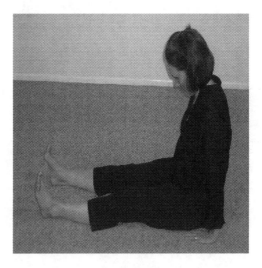

You will now perform what is basically the Table Pose in yoga. As you inhale, lift your buttocks off of the ground and allow your head to drop back. The final position of this movement should be where your legs are bent at a right angle at the knees with your feet on the ground, your abdomen and chest parallel to the ground, your arms straight, and your head tilted back so that you are looking at what is behind you upside down.

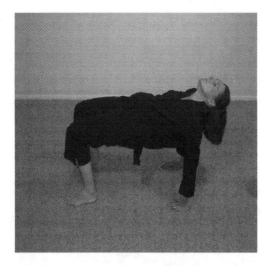

In this position, hold your breath and perform a full-body isometric - tensing all of your muscles. After a moment of this tensing, as you exhale, relax all of your muscles and allow your body to come down into the original posture, with your behind on the ground, your chin on your chest. Repeat the desired number of times, eventually working up to 21. Then sit comfortably with your eyes closed, observing body sensations, allowing your breath to return to normal.

This exercise tones the abdominal muscles and organs and energizes the region of the solar plexus. *Prana* or life force is driven deep into the body as a result of isometric tensing.

As this is a strenuous exercise, remember to maintain regular and balanced breathing. Slow down or pause if you become winded. Two other difficulties that people report in doing this exercise are pains in the shoulders and an inability to bring the torso to the parallel position. Regarding the first, unless you have a rotator cuff or other specific shoulder or upper arm complaint, the pain experienced during or after is a beneficial structural adjustment to performing the exercise. But, do not push hard when you meet resistance and if there is pain, be a bit gentler in coming up to the position, allowing the action to feel more comfortable. If pain persists for longer than a week, it is advisable to consult a health professional (massage or physical therapist). Also, if you have a specific shoulder complaint, you may find that a lower number of repetitions of this exercise promote faster healing.

As regards the second difficulty, where one cannot bring oneself up for the torso and legs to be parallel with the ground, this often arises from weak abdominal and lower back muscles. Try to lift yourself up to the best of your ability. And, as mentioned earlier, visualize yourself moving into the perfect position whilst performing the exercise.

Exercise #5

This exercise is similar to Upward and Downward Facing Dog, but more dynamic.

Place yourself into a push-up type position with both your hands and feet spread about two feet apart. Your toes should be curled (not pointed back) and back sagged so that curvature of your spine allows you to be looking forward. You are holding your body slightly off the ground with your hands and toes. Not even your knees or any other part of your hips or legs should touch the ground.

As you inhale, drop your head and shoulders towards the ground and raise your behind so that you are looking between your own legs. Your behind should be higher than any other part of your body. As you exhale, reverse this flow so that you lower yourself down into the original position. Repeat this for a number of times that feels comfortable, working up to 21. At the completion of this exercise, stand erect with your hands on your hips, inhaling through the nose and out through the mouth a few times until your breath returns to normal. Allow your entire body to relax.

The arching of the entire spine in this exercise rejuvenates the nerves in the spine and improves the functioning of the immune system. Both the arms and legs are also strengthened.

This can be a difficult posture, especially for those who either have weak abdominal muscles or suffer from low back complaints. Of course, this exercise will help such conditions, but it may be necessary to initially modify the exercise to prevent more strain or injury. The following modifications I have found to be useful and still provide positive results.

The first posture is where you <u>do</u> allow your knees to rest on the ground. You arch forward as best you can, at least trying to look before you. In what would be the Downward Facing Dog posture where behind would be up, here, as you inhale, you draw yourself back onto your haunches, providing a good stretch to the entire spine and your hips. Then, as you exhale, you come of your haunches and return to the original modified position.

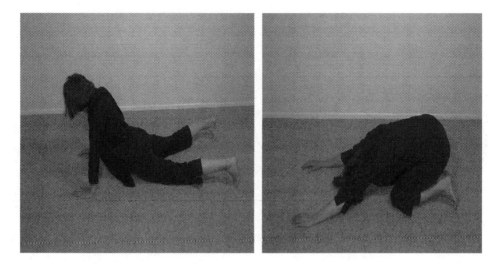

These five are the foundation of Tibetan Rejuvenation Exercises. For such a short and simple series, the benefits of their practice are very rewarding - on physical, psychological, and spiritual levels. Once one becomes proficient in these five, there is an additional, more esoteric practice that one can learn about by referring to *Tibetan Ayurveda*. But, even without adding this component, these five will promote greater mental and physical flexibility and openness and you will experience a state of being that is radiant and joyful; a reflection of true rejuvenation.

SOURCE APPENDIX

Please note that the listing of products is not exhaustive. Nor is it a particular recommendation for you to choose these companies or products over and above others you may be able to source for yourself. The idea here is to get you on the road to discovering what will be helpful for your rest and sleep.

Ergonomic Mattresses:
Useful article: http://www.spineuniverse.com/wellness/sleep/mattresses-matter-ergonomic-guidelines

Sattva
http://www.saatvamattress.com

Magnetic Mattresses:
ProMagnet.com
MagneticMattressCovers.com
http://www.magneticmattresscovers.com/
Absolute Comfort
http://www.absolutecomfortonsale.com
Nikken USA
http://www.nikkenusa.com

Egg Crate Mattress Pads:
Foam Order
https://www.foamorder.com

parent giving
http://www.parentgiving.com

Down pillows:
PacificCoast.com
https://www.pacificcoast.com/
The Company Store
http://www.thecompanystore.com

Ergonomic pillows:
Relax The Back
http://www.relaxtheback.com/pillows.html
Essentia
http://www.myessentia.com/pillows/ergonomic
Ai Sleep Direct
http://www.aisleepdirect.com

Magnetic Pillows:
ProMagnet.com
http://www.promagnet.com
Therion
http://www.therionmagnetics.com

Far Infrared Blankets and Comforters:
Nikken USA
http://www.nikkenusa.com

Sleep Enhancement Pillows:
from Diamond Way Ayurveda (http://www.DiamondWayAyurveda.com)
Tummy Warmer – heat-able pillow for warmth on belly, feet, etc...
Cool Eyes – eye pad

Herbal Pillows:
Wellcat.com
EMF Shielding Technology:

Tools for Wellness (source for wall plugs, room EMF shields, and negative ion generators)
http://www.toolsforwellness.com
Qi Mag products (to address geopathic stress, water lines, etc...)
http://www.feng-shui.com/en/feng-shui.html

Helpful CDs and DVDs for Rest, Relaxation, and Sleep

"Dreamscapes Music for Deep Sleep" by Krista Lee Orman (NOTE: really brilliant and effective)

"Journeys Into Bliss" by Robert Sachs, Diamond Way Ayurveda (DVD with continuous play tracks) Available through www.DiamondWayAyurveda.com

"Yoga Nidra and Self Healing: the Art of Conscious Deep Relaxation" by Dr. Marc Halpern

https://www.amazon.com/

BOOKS:

Fretwell, Sally. *Feng Shui: Back to Balance*. New World Library, Novato, CA.

Lusk, Julie. Yoga Nidra for Complete Relaxation and Stress Relief. ISBN-13: 978-1626251823 ISBN-10: 1626251827

Sachs, Melanie. *Ayurvedic Beauty Care*. (Lotus Press, Twin Lakes, WI, 1994)

Sachs, Melanie and Robert. *Ayurvedic Spa*. (Lotus Books, Twin Lakes, WI, 2007)

Sachs, Robert. *Tibetan Ayurveda*. (Inner Traditions/Bear and Company, Rochester, VT, 2001)

And, to take the idea of sleep and dreams to a whole new understanding, consider reading...

Wangyal Rinpoche, Tenzin. *The Tibetan Yogas of Dreams and Sleep*. (Snow Lion Publications, Ithaca, NY. 1998)

Yamamoto, Shizuko. *Barefoot Shiatsu*. Japan Publications, Inc., Tokyo and New York 1978

Printed in the United States
by Baker & Taylor Publisher Services